Contents

What is the environment?

The environment is the world all around us.

Help the Environment

ing

ter

Guillain

nann
LIBRARY

www.heinemannlibrary.co.uk
Visit our website to find out more information about Heinemann Library books.

To order:
☎ Phone 44 (0) 1865 888066
📄 Send a fax to 44 (0) 1865 314091
💻 Visit the Heinemann Bookshop at www.heinemannlibrary.co.uk to browse our catalogue and order online.

Heinemann Library is an imprint of Capstone Global Library Limited, a company incorporated in England and Wales having its registered office at 7 Pilgrim Street, London, EC4V 6LB – Registered company number: 6695582

Heinemann is a registered trademark of Pearson Education Limited, under licence to Capstone Global Library Limited

Editorial: Sian Smith and Cassie Mayer
Design: Philippa Jenkins
Picture research: Erica Martin, Hannah Taylor and Ginny Stroud-Lewis
Production: Duncan Gilbert

Printed and bound in China by South China Printing Co. Ltd.

ISBN 978 0 431 19217 8 (hardback)
12 11 10 09 08
10 9 8 7 6 5 4 3 2 1

ISBN 978 0 431 19223 9 (paperback)
13 12 11 10 09
10 9 8 7 6 5 4 3 2 1

British Library Cataloguing in Publication Data
Guillain, Charlotte
  Saving water. - (Help the environment) (Acorn)
  1. Water conservation - Juvenile literature 2. Water reuse
  - Juvenile literature
  I. Title
  333.9'116

Acknowledgements
The publishers would like to thank the following for permission to reproduce photographs: ©Alamy pp. **16** (Bjanka Kadic), **4 bottom left** (Kevin Foy), **17** (Keith M Law), **4 top right**, **23** (Westend 61); ©ardea. com pp. **19** (Jean Michel Labat), **15** (Mark Boulton); ©Brand X Pixtures pp. **4 bottom right**, **21** (Morey Milbradt); ©Corbis pp. **8**, **10** (Randy Faris), **9**, **12** (zefa, Grace); ©Digital Vision p. **4 top left**; ©Getty Images pp. **14** (AFP, Liu Jin, Staff), **13** (medioImages); ©Jupiter Images p. **22** (Polka Dot Images); ©Photoeditinc. p. **5** (Michael Newman); ©Photolibrary pp. **7** (Botanica), **11** (Image 100), **18** (Photoalto), **20** (Radius Images), **6** (Photodisc)

Cover photograph of tap reproduced with permission of ©Fancy (Punchstock). Back cover photograph of a boy washing up reproduced with permission of ©Corbis (zefa, Grace).

Every effort has been made to contact copyright holders of any material reproduced in this book. Any omissions will be rectified in subsequent printings if notice is given to the publishers.

We need to care for
the environment.

How do we use water?

We use water for many things.

When we save water, we
help the environment.

Ways to help the environment

We use water to wash dishes.

We save water if we turn off the
tap while we wash up.
We are helping the environment.

We use water when we brush
our teeth.

We save water if we turn off the
tap while we brush our teeth.
We are helping the environment.

We use water to wash our bodies.

We save water if we take a
shower instead of a bath.
We are helping the environment.

We waste water if a tap is dripping.

We save water if we fix a
dripping tap.
We are helping the environment.

Plants need water to grow.

catches rainwater

We save water if we catch
rainwater to water plants.
We are helping the environment. 17

A hose uses lots of water.

We save water if we use a
watering can instead of a hose.
We are helping the environment.

We can save water.

We can help the environment.

How are they helping?

How is this child saving water?

Answer on p. 24

Picture glossary

environment the world around us

Index

Answer to question on p.22: He is washing a car using a bucket of water instead of a hose.

Note to Parents and Teachers

Before reading

Talk to children about all the ways we use water (drinking, washing, eating, growing things, etc.). Explain that in many places in the world, people do not have clean water that comes out of a tap in their houses. We need to save water and not waste it.

After reading

Draw a cross-section of a house and divide it into rooms upstairs and downstairs. Label each room: bathroom, bedroom, kitchen, living room. Ask children to think of ways they can save water in each room (e.g. bathroom – turning off the tap while brushing teeth).